Far-Fetched Pets

YOUR
PET
BEAVER

By Bobbie Hamsa
Illustrations by Tom Dunnington

Consultant:
  James P. Rowan
  Keeper, Small Mammal House
  Lincoln Park Zoo, Chicago

 CHILDRENS PRESS, CHICAGO

CAUTION

Far-fetched pets should not be kept in your house or apartment or yard. Don't ask for one for your birthday or Christmas. Go to the zoo or visit the library. There you can learn more about your favorite far-fetched pet.

Library of Congress Cataloging in Publication Data

Hamsa, Bobbie.
  Your pet beaver.

  (Far-fetched pets)
  SUMMARY: Lists the many pleasures of having a beaver for a pet, including his abilities to cut firewood, swat flies, and shape hamburger patties.
  [1. Beavers—Anecdotes, facetiae, satire, etc.]
I. Dunnington, Tom. II. Title. III. Series.
PZ7.H1887Yo   [E]   79-23379
ISBN 0-516-03352-2

PZ7.H1887Ye

1 2 3 4 5 6 7 8 9 10 11 12 R 88 87 86 85 84 83 82 81 80

111553

This is a beaver.
An American beaver.
Pretend that he is your pet.

He has reddish-brown fur.

Big tough teeth that never need brushing.

A flat strong tail.

And two webbed feet as big as your hands.

What will you name your pet beaver?

CARE AND FEEDING OF YOUR PET

Beavers eat plants, grass, leaves, herbs, weeds, buds, and flowers.

Each day give him two pounds of aspen bark and some water lily waffles.

Otherwise, he'll eat your garden.

Grooming a beaver is rather fun.

Once a week or so, take a few drops of musk grease (he'll make it for you) and carefully comb it into his fur.

Make sure you get the sides real slick. And put plenty on his belly.

Now he is totally waterproof.
And terribly handsome, besides.

Your beaver will need a big, wet place to live.

Perhaps you have a swimming pool?

Or a stream running under your window?

If not, buy a leaky water bed.

Or put a horse tank in your room.

IMPORTANT NOTE:

A beaver can't be truly happy unless there's plenty of water around.

And, he's not very keen on sunshine.

So if you live in the desert, choose another pet.

If he's young, he's a beaver kit.
(You don't have to put him together.
That's just what they call baby beavers.)

A beaver is a nice-sized pet to have.

He won't grow any bigger than you are right now.

So he fits nicely into back seats, red wagons, and baby buggies.

Where will you put your pet beaver?

Your beaver is a lot like you—
clean, polite, friendly.
And brave.
But he *is* afraid of coyotes.
Coyotes eat beavers.
So do wolves, wolverines, and lynx.

You'll notice your beaver rests all day.
And fools around all night.
That's nice.
Because if you can't get to sleep,
you'll have an instant playmate.

Your pet likes exercise.
He's very good at "Pick-Up-Sticks."
He's a pretty passable ping-pong player.
And he loves all water sports,
especially "Submarine."

He can't climb, though.
So keep him off the monkey bars.

TRAINING

Your beaver is eager to make himself useful.
Cracking nuts . . .
repairing fallen plaster . . .
making mud pies . . .

spanking naughty dolls . . .
and shaping hamburgers for Mom.
(Wash his tail first.)

He can swat flies on the patio . . .
and flatten your pillow when it's
too fat to sleep on.

His teeth come in handy, too.
Cutting firewood for Dad . . .
winning smile contests . . .

ripping cardboard off plastic-wrapped toys . . .
manicuring Mom's nails . . .
and taking your place at the dentist.

Because he's waterproof, he can run errands
when it's raining . . .
change the sprinkler hose for Dad . . .
fix leaky faucets . . .
and tell you when your shower's ready.

Your beaver can be many things.
A can opener . . .
a foot warmer . . .
a room cleaner.

But best of all, he can build you the
biggest, strongest, most wonderful play
house the world has ever seen . . .
with many rooms . . .
deep, dark tunnels . . .
secret doors . . .
hiding places.
And your very own pond to swim in.

These are only a few of the things
your pet beaver can do.
Can you think of more?

If you take good care of him, your
beaver will live maybe 20 years.
And you'll say he's the best pet
you ever had.

Facts about your pet American Beaver *(Castor canadensis)*

Number of newborn: 2, born in the spring

Average size when grown: up to 3 feet tall, up to 60 pounds in weight

Type of food eaten: bark and shoots of willows, poplars, alders, etc.; also aquatic plants (water lilies, etc.)

Expected lifespan: 15 to 20 years

Names:—male: none
female: none
young: kit or pup
group: family or colony

Where found: Originally, all of the northern half of North America. Has been re-introduced to some areas of its former range and is making a come back (after being nearly exterminated by fur trappers in the nineteenth century).

About the Author:

Bobbie Hamsa was born and raised in Nebraska, far away from any far-fetched pets. Mrs. Hamsa has a Bachelor of Arts Degree in English Literature from the University of Nebraska. She is married and has a son, John.

Mrs. Hamsa is an advertising copywriter in Omaha. She writes print, radio, and television copy for a full range of accounts, including Mutual of Omaha's "Wild Kingdom," the five-time Emmy Award winning wild animal series and sometime resource for far-fetched pets.

About the Artist:

Tom Dunnington divides his time between book illustration and wildlife painting. He has done many books for Childrens Press, as well as working on textbooks, and is a regular contributor to "Highlights for Children." Tom lives in Oak Park, Illinois.